Flower Your Garden

By Shiela M. Keaise
Illustrated by 26 Colleton County Youths

Colleton County Memorial Library
Children's Department
4th Illustrate-A-Book (IAB) Project

The fourth book, Flower Your Garden, *in the Illustrate-A-Book Program is dedicated to our front cover winner, Alondra DeSantiago, who has been published three times in the IAB Project, and Paul Murray, the back cover winner.*

Summary of Book:
Flower Your Garden looks at different types of flowers that would be great for any garden, but Ms. Shiela includes rhyme and tools that are essential to keep the flowers growing and story going.

Text copyright ©2009 by Shiela M. Keaise
Illustrations copyright ©2009 by Colleton County Memorial Library
All rights reserved
600 Hampton Street, Walterboro, SC 29488
www.colletonlibrary.org

[1.Flowers—Literature.] I. Title.
ISBN-13: 978-0-6158829-0-1
ISBN-10: 0-6158829-0-0

Printed in the United States of America
August 2009

Planting a flower requires a few basic rules.

Rules
For
Planting
your
garden

Maintaining your garden requires a few basic tools.

Begin your garden with our state's Yellow Jessamine today.

Then plant other flowers and use these devices without delay.

A sod cutter and tiller maybe just the right mix.

Planting Oriental Poppy is one of the best picks.

A hoe loosens the ground and helps with this gardener's deed.

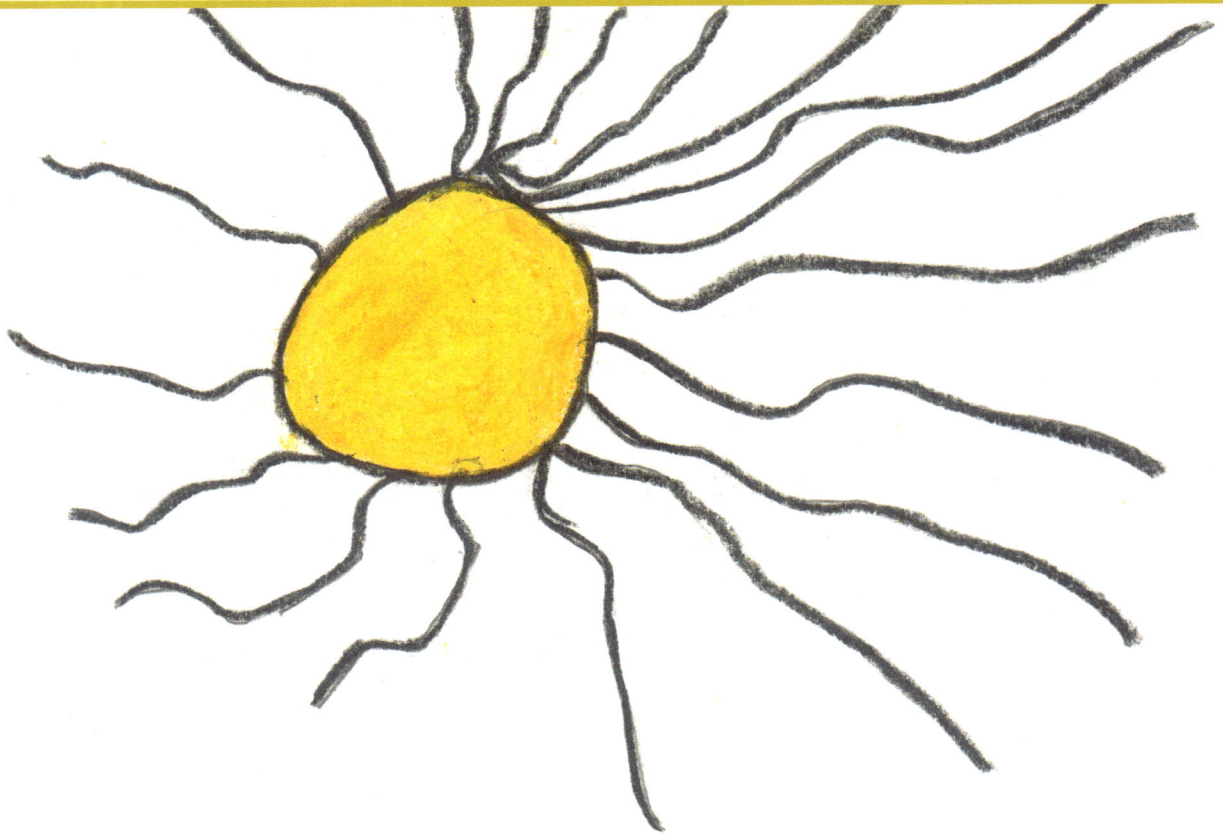

Only in rich woods and rocky slopes grows the Star Chickweed.

A hand trowel may help when digging smaller holes.

By planting Brown-Eyed Susan, you can reach your goals.

A garden glove protects your hand this is true.

Try planting the Stemmed Golden Rod painted blue.

A garden rake is right for planting new bought seeds.

In moist soil you can enjoy most Hedge Bindweeds.

A wheelbarrow or garden cart can add in the mulch.

It takes a special hand to maintain the Jerusalem Artichoke.

A narrow, sharp, flat spade adds to the gardener's story.

Throughout the year you will like seeing the Morning Glory.

A pruner comes in a variety of shapes and sizes.

It is fun to watch the Azalea fall but it soon rises.

A shear is good for most flowers you choose.

Without it the Rose would cause you to bruise.

Use the right garden tools if you desire to be smart.

You will be a good flower gardener from the heart.

Flower your garden with all kinds of beautiful plants.

Then we can enjoy flowers in the wind as they dance.

Flowers to Know

Yellow Jessamine, page 4

Oriental Poppy, page 7

Star Chickweed, page 9

Brown-Eyed Susan, page 11

Blue-Stemmed Golden Rod, page 13

Hedge Bindweeds, page 15

Jerusalem Artichoke, page 17

Morning Glory, page 19

Azalea, page 21

Rose, page 23

Flower Your Garden

Planting a flower requires a few basic rules.
Maintaining your garden requires a few basic tools.

Begin your garden with our state's Yellow Jessamine today.
Then plant other flowers and use these devices without delay.

A sod cutter and tiller maybe just the right mix.
Planting Oriental Poppy is one of the best picks.

A hoe loosens the ground and helps with this gardener's deed.
Only in rich woods and rocky slopes grows the Star Chickweed.

A hand trowel may help when digging smaller holes.
By planting Brown-Eyed Susan, you can reach your goals.

A garden glove protects your hand this is true.
Try planting the Stemmed Golden Rod painted blue.

A garden rake is right for planting new bought seeds.
In moist soil you can enjoy most Hedge Bindweeds.

A wheelbarrow or garden cart can add in the mulch.
It takes a special hand to maintain the Jerusalem Artichoke.

A narrow, sharp, flat spade adds to the gardener's story.
Throughout the year you will like seeing the Morning Glory.

A pruner comes in a variety of shapes and sizes.
It is fun to watch the Azalea fall but it soon rises.

A shear is good for most flowers you choose.
Without it the Rose would cause you to bruise.

Use the right garden tools if you desire to be smart.
You will be a good flower gardener from the heart.

Flower your garden with all kinds of beautiful plants.
Then we can enjoy flowers in the wind as they dance.

Colleton County Memorial Library
Children's Department
2008 Best Illustrator Contest Winners &
4th Illustrate-A-Book Project Participants

SCHOOL	WINNER	AGE	PAGE #
Bells Elementary	Erin Langdale	8	7
Black Street Elementary	Rodgrick Geathers	12	3
	Shawn Haltiwanger	11	5
	Terrance Clark	10	13
Adult Education	Lakara Thompson	18	21
Colleton Middle	Eva Ferguson	13	10
	Tyler Grant	13	11
	Paul Murray	12	12
Forest Circle Middle (13 winners)	Emmie Faulk	13	6
	Jacqueline Lippold	12	14
	Kelsey Barnes	12	15
	Whitney Westbury	13	17
	Cyrus Legree	14	18
	Mari Garris	12	19
	Sierra Britt	11	20
	Khadaijah Gillison	14	22
	Jessica Hickman	13	23
	Mary Thibodeau	11	25
	Alondra DeSantiago	13	26
	Alexandra Lawrinowicz	14	27
Forest Hills Elementary	Christopher Reyes	6	8
	Gloria Kim	8	24
Home School	Lacey Helton	11	2
	Emily Wand	11	4
	Abigail Drake	10	9
	Harrison Wand	9	16

Colleton County Memorial Library
Children's Department
4th Illustrate-A-Book Project Judges

NAME	OCCUPATION	PAGE #
Jami Gahagan	System Tech Librarian	2
Bridget Murray	Fabric Artist	3
Cherry Keaise	Teacher	4
Suhailah Beyah	Teacher	5
Ellen Capers	Library Staff	6
Jingle Valentine	Parent	7
Joyce Chaplin	Bookmobile Librarian	8
Edward Vanhorn	Custodian	9
Casey Beard	High School Student	10
Elflorence Oliver	Citizen	11
Allan Badger	Published Illustrator	12
Betty Hurlbutt	Library Patron	13
Willie Rabb	Retired Teacher	14
Heather Whitten	Art Teacher	15
Carl Coffin	Assistant Director of Library	16
Edwin Merwin	University Librarian	17
Lorna Triplett	Teacher	18
Lakara Thompson	Library Volunteer	19
Jane Shaw	Assistant Bookmobile Librarian	20
Jeanne Langston	Art Teacher	21
Jennie Oliver	Parent	22
Brian Blake	Reference Librarian	23
Linda Gottschalk	Citizen	24
Travis Godley	President of Friends of CCML	25
Sharon Williams	Teacher	26
Al'Leigh Murray	Published Illustrator	27

Do You Know The Illustrators?

NAME/AGE	PAGE
Lacey Helton, Age 11	Page 2
Rodgrick Geathers, Age 12	Page 3
Emily Wand, Age 11	Page 4
Shawn Haltiwanger, Age 11	Page 5
Emmie Faulk, Age 13	Page 6
Erin Langdale, Age 8	Page 7
Christopher Reyes, Age 6	Page 8
Abigail Drake, Age 10	Page 9
Eva Ferguson, Age 13	Page 10
Tyler Grant, Age 13	Page 11
Paul Murray, Age 12	Page 12
Terrance Clark, Age 10	Page 13
Jacqueline Lippold, Age 12	Page 14
Kelsey Barnes, Age 12	Page 15
Harrison Wand, Age 9	Page 16
Whitney Westbury, Age 13	Page 17
Cyrus Legree, Age 14	Page 18
Mari Garris, Age 12	Page 19
Sierra Britt, Age 11	Page 20
Lakara Thompson, Age 18	Page 21
Khadaijah Gillison, Age 14	Page 22
Jessica Hickman, Age 13	Page 23
Gloria Kim, Age 8	Page 24
Mary Thibodeau, Age 11	Page 25
Alondra DeSantiago, Age 13	Page 26
Alexandra Lawrinowicz, Age 14	Page 27

Do You Know The Author?

Shiela M. Keaise is the Children's Librarian at the Colleton County Memorial Library. Ms. Shiela is also a storyteller, certified child care trainer, and author of three of the Illustrate-A-Book projects and *Hannah and Dexter: The First Meeting*, illustrated by Najah Clemmons. She started the Illustrate-A-Book program with hopes of sharing the talents of the artistic volunteers and gifted children.

www.ingramcontent.com/pod-product-compliance
Lightning Source LLC
Chambersburg PA
CBHW041428090426
42741CB00002B/76